How To Do Discrete Trial Training

PRO-ED Series on Autism Spectrum Disorders

Edited by Richard L. Simpson

Titles in the Series

PRO-ED Series on Autism Spectrum Disorders

How To Do
Discrete Trial Training

Sonja R. de Boer

pro·ed
An International Publisher

8700 Shoal Creek Boulevard
Austin, Texas 78757-6897
800/897-3202   Fax 800/397-7633
www.proedinc.com

© 2007 by PRO-ED, Inc.
8700 Shoal Creek Boulevard
Austin, Texas 78757-6897
800/897-3202 Fax 800/397-7633
www.proedinc.com

Library of Congress Cataloging-in-Publication Data

de Boer, Sonja R.
   How to do discrete trial training / Sonja R. DeBoer; edited by Richard L. Simpson.
      p. cm. — (PRO-ED series on autism spectrum disorders)
      Includes bibliographical references.
      ISBN 1-4164-0145-8 (softcover : alk. paper)
      1. Autistic children—Education.   2. Autistic children—Behavior modification.
   3. Learning. I. Title. II. Series.
LC4717.D43 2006
371.94—dc22

                                                                    2005035702

Art Director: Jason Crosier
Designer: Nancy McKinney
This book is designed in Nexus Serif TF and Neutra Text.

Printed in the United States of America

8 9 10 11 12 13   22 21 20 19 18 17

Contents

About Autism Spectrum Disorders

Autism spectrum disorders (ASD) are complex, neurologically based developmental disabilities that typically appear early in life. The Autism Society of America (2004) estimates that as many as 1.5 million people in the United States have autism or some form of pervasive developmental disorder. Indeed, its prevalence makes ASD an increasingly common and currently the fastest-growing developmental disability. ASD are perplexing and enigmatic. According to the *Diagnostic and Statistical Manual of Mental Disorders,* individuals with ASD have difficulty in interacting normally with others; exhibit speech, language, and communication difficulties (e.g., delayed speech, echolalia); insist on routines and environmental uniformity; engage in self-stimulatory and stereotypic behaviors; and respond atypically to sensory stimuli (American Psychiatric Association, 2000; Simpson & Myles, 1998). In some cases, aggressive and self-injurious behavior may be present in these individuals. Yet, in tandem with these characteristics, children with ASD often have normal patterns of physical growth and development, a wide range of cognitive and language capabilities, and some individuals with ASD have highly developed and unique abilities (Klin, Volkmar, & Sparrow, 2000). These widely varied characteristics necessitate specially designed interventions and strategies orchestrated by knowledgeable and skilled professionals.

Preface to the Series

Teaching and managing learners with ASD can be demanding, but favorable outcomes for children and youth with autism and autism-related disabilities depend on professionals using appropriate and valid methods in their education. Because identifying and correctly using effective teaching methods is often enormously challenging (National Research Council, 2001; Simpson et al., 2005), it is the intent of this series to provide professionals with scientifically based methods for intervention. Each book in the series is designed to assist professionals and parents in choosing and correctly using a variety of interventions that have the potential to produce significant benefits for children and youth with ASD. Written in a user-friendly, straightforward fashion by qualified and experienced professionals, the books are aimed at individuals who seek practical solutions and strategies for successfully working with learners with ASD.

Richard L. Simpson
Series Editor

References

American Psychiatric Association. (2000). *Diagnostic and statistical manual of mental disorders* (4th ed., text rev.). Washington, DC: Author.

Autism Society of America. (2004). *What is autism?* Retrieved March 11, 2005, from http://autism-society.org

Klin, A., Volkmar, F., & Sparrow, S. (2000). *Asperger syndrome.* New York: Guilford Press.

National Research Council. (2001). *Educating children with autism.* Committee on Educational Interventions for Children with Autism, Division of Behavioral and Social Sciences and Education. Washington, DC: National Academy Press.

Simpson, R., de Boer-Ott, S., Griswold, D., Myles, B., Byrd, S., Ganz, J., et al. (2005). *Autism spectrum disorders: Interventions and treatments for children and youth.* Thousand Oaks, CA: Corwin Press.

Simpson, R. L., & Myles, B. S. (1998). *Educating children and youth with autism: Strategies for effective practice.* Austin, TX: PRO-ED.

Introduction

To be able to use the discrete trial teaching (DTT) method with students with autism spectrum disorders (ASD), it is important for the reader to first have an understanding of the disability itself. The brief description that follows will ensure that all who read this manual understand the definition of ASD and the foundation it provides for the use of DTT.

ASD falls under the American Psychiatric Association umbrella of pervasive developmental disabilities (PDD). Children who are diagnosed with a pervasive developmental disorder exhibit "severe and pervasive impairments in several areas of development: reciprocal social interactions skills, communication skills, or the presence of stereotyped behavior, interests, and activities" (American Psychiatric Association [APA], 2000, p. 64). This PDD classification consists of the following: autistic disorder (a.k.a. autism); pervasive developmental disorder–not otherwise specified (PDD-NOS); Asperger syndrome; Rett's disorder; and childhood disintegrative disorder.

Individuals who are diagnosed with pervasive developmental disabilities according to the diagnostic criteria of the *Diagnostic and Statistical Manual of Mental Disorders,* 4th ed. (APA, 2000) do not necessarily behave or function similarly. Those with *autism* typically exhibit the most severe cognitive and language impairments compared to other individuals with ASD. Those diagnosed with Asperger syndrome exhibit the least severe communication and cognitive impairments. Those diagnosed with PDD-NOS often display many of the same speech–language and cognitive patterns as those with autism, albeit typically in less severe forms.

One common characteristic among individuals with ASD is their unbalanced pattern of skill development (Burack & Volkmar, 1992; Committee on Educational Interventions for Children with Autism, 2001; Van Meter, Fein, Morris, Waterhouse, & Allen, 1997). For instance, an individual with ASD may display math skills several years beyond his age yet may be unable to use the toilet independently. In this connection individuals who teach and plan skill development programs for learners with ASD, including professionals and parents, typically consider the following skill domains: (a) cognition, (b) learning, (c) social interaction, (d) play, (e) communication, (f) adaptive behavior, (g) behavior, (h) motor, and (i) sensory sensitivities (Atwood, 1998; Koegel, Koegel, Frea, & Smith, 1995; Mauk, Reber, & Batshaw,

1997; Myles & Simpson, 2003). Related to these domains, this manual provides information on teaching skills to children and youth with ASD via the method of discrete trial teaching.

To assist readers in understanding and using the DTT method, the following information is provided:

- a brief description of applied behavior analysis (ABA) as it relates to DTT and ASD;
- a brief description of the antecedent, behavior, and consequence paradigm;
- a description of the concepts imbedded in the structure of the DTT paradigm;
- a list and description of teaching concepts and skills needed to provide a structured teaching environment for using DTT with students with ASD; and
- a glossary of terms.

Examples and practice exercises are also provided to help readers gain an understanding of the concepts and skills that form the foundation for DTT.

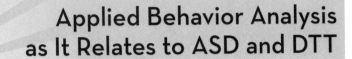

Applied Behavior Analysis as It Relates to ASD and DTT

Applied behavior analysis (ABA) is the process of systematically applying the principles of behavior to "improve socially significant behavior to a meaningful degree and to demonstrate experimentally" that the procedures used were actually responsible for the change (improvement) in the behavior (Cooper, Heron, & Heward, 1987, p. 14). Accordingly, an instructor *applies* behavior principles in order to change an individual's *behavior* and then *analyzes* whether the actions taken caused a behavior to change. A crucial component of ABA is the process of *improving the social significance* of the individual's behavior. That is, it is important that the change in behavior be observable, meaningful, and important, such as teaching an individual to read, add and subtract numbers, not hit other people, follow a teacher's instructions, or improve her social acceptance within her community.

A significant amount of scientifically based research on ABA has been conducted, and no other intervention method has proven more effective with individuals with ASD (Simpson et al., 2004). Studies have demonstrated that using ABA intervention methods with individuals with ASD can produce comprehensive and lasting improvements in many important skill areas, including language, academics, behavior, and social interaction. Behavior analysts view ASD as a "syndrome of behavioral deficits and excesses that have a neurological basis but are nonetheless amenable to change in response to specific, carefully programmed, constructive interactions within the environment" (Green, 1996, pp. 29–30). Because individuals with ASD do not respond to their environment in the same manner as nondisabled persons, they do not readily learn and respond to typical instruction. The ABA intervention methods offer instructors a systematic process for teaching skills in small units in a way that allows individuals with ASD to understand and learn. Discrete trial teaching is one specific way of using ABA to teach children and youth with ASD.

The Antecedent, Behavior, and Consequence Paradigm

The antecedent, behavior, and consequence (ABC) paradigm (Cooper et al., 1987) is a fundamental concept within ABA and DTT. All ABA procedures involve the manipulation of one or more components of this three-term contingency plan:

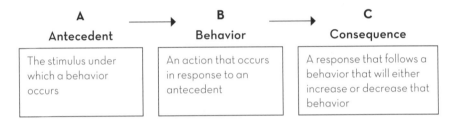

A Antecedent	B Behavior	C Consequence
The stimulus under which a behavior occurs	An action that occurs in response to an antecedent	A response that follows a behavior that will either increase or decrease that behavior

This ABC paradigm allows analysis of behavior that is occurring in *any* environment. By recording the occurrence of a behavior and the events that occurred immediately before and after the behavior, one is able to evaluate the cause (antecedent) and effect (consequence) of a behavior. By using a data collection system to maintain a record of the behavior, along with the antecedents and consequences of each occurrence, one is able to track and analyze patterns that occur and thus more accurately instruct a learner in a new skill and otherwise intervene to increase or decrease the occurrence of the behavior. Examples of the ABC paradigm follow:

Reinforcement of Appropriate Behavior

A: Adult is holding a cookie within view of a child.

B: Child asks adult, "Cookie, please?"

C: Adult gives the child the cookie.

Reinforcement of Inappropriate Behavior

A: Adult is holding a cookie within view of a child.

B: Child throws a tantrum and tries to take cookie from adult.

C: Adult gives the child the cookie.

These two examples include the same antecedent and the same consequence, but the child is displaying and being reinforced for different behaviors. In the first example, the child asks for the cookie appropriately, and the adult gives it to him; in the second, the child inappropriately throws a tantrum and tries to take the cookie from the adult, and the adult gives it to him. An instructor can view these data and see that in the future, the first child will most likely continue to appropriately ask for things that he wants, and the second child will continue to try to grab things from people or throw a tantrum when he wants something.

Important information can be gained by using the ABC paradigm to analyze behaviors. ABC data are very useful in revealing why a behavior occurs and in what situations it is most likely to occur again. These data can also reveal what consequences are causing a behavior to increase or decrease and, therefore, help instructors determine appropriate consequences to use in the future.

Using the Discrete Trial Method To Teach Skills

Understanding the structure and use of the three-part ABC paradigm is essential to understanding and using DTT and maximizing an individual's learning. This method of teaching involves the following:

- breaking a skill into smaller parts,
- teaching each part to mastery,
- providing concentrated teaching,
- providing prompting and fading as necessary, and
- using reinforcement procedures.

Each DTT teaching session involves a number of trials, each of which has a distinct beginning and end, hence the term *discrete*. The DTT method is distinguishable from traditional teaching methods because it prescribes presenting a very small unit of information and immediately seeking the student's response. Active instructor and student involvement is an element of DTT.

The DTT method mirrors the ABC paradigm as follows:

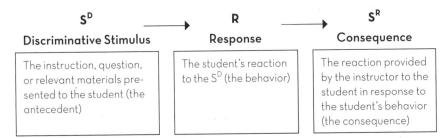

S^D	R	S^R
Discriminative Stimulus	**Response**	**Consequence**
The instruction, question, or relevant materials presented to the student (the antecedent)	The student's reaction to the S^D (the behavior)	The reaction provided by the instructor to the student in response to the student's behavior (the consequence)

Just as the ABC paradigm is used to analyze a behavior that a student is demonstrating, the DTT method is a more narrowly focused paradigm for analyzing the learning behavior of a student. Each DTT element is recorded: the instruction provided (antecedent), the student's response (behavior), and the instructor's response to the student (consequence). This basic DTT process enables one to evaluate the cause (antecedent) and effect (consequence) of a student's learning. Using a data collection system that assists in maintaining a record of a student's responses to specific instructions and the consequences that follow those responses, an instructor can track and analyze the effects of instruction (and specific materials) and consequences and thus ultimately increase or decrease the occurrence of specific responses of the student with greater accuracy. Three examples of different ways, both appropriate and inappropriate, to increase or decrease the occurrence of a specific response follow:

Reinforcement of Appropriate Response (increases response):

S^D: Instructor says, "Give me sock." [A sock is lying on the floor in front of the student.]

R: Student picks up the sock and hands it to the instructor.

S^R: Instructor says, "All right! Good job," and tickles the student, who laughs in response.

No Reinforcement of Inappropriate Response (decreases response):

S^D: Instructor says, "Give me sock."

R: Student looks around the room and does nothing.

S^R: Instructor says, "Let's try again."

Reinforcement of Inappropriate Response (increases response):

S^D: Instructor says, "Give me sock."

R: Student looks around the room and does nothing.

S^R: Instructor says, "Come on, Johnny. Here is the sock—see it?" and tickles the student, who laughs in response.

The first example presents an instructor appropriately reinforcing a student for a correct response. Accordingly, in the future, the student is more likely to correctly identify a sock. The second example presents an instructor appropriately not reinforcing the student's failure to respond to the instruction. Therefore, the instructor has decreased the likelihood of the student not responding in the future. The third example presents an instructor *in*appropriately reinforcing the student for not responding to the instruction. Even though the student did not respond correctly to the instruction, the instructor reinforced him. Therefore, in the future, the student is more likely not to respond to an instruction, because he has learned that he may still receive reinforcement.

There are two important reasons to use DTT with students with ASD. First, because students with ASD do not naturally gain information from their environment by observing and listening to others or modeling others' behavior, the DTT method enables instructors to systematically analyze tasks that a student needs to learn, break them down into small, defined steps, and systematically teach them to a student in incremental elements that he can more easily learn. This method also enables different teachers to be consistent in their instruction by clearly writing out the procedures for implementing a discrete trial (S^D—R—S^R). This strategy assists teaching consistency—in instructional language, presentation of the S^D, and application of consequences—thereby facilitating student learning. It also allows instructors to more easily and more accurately collect data, because the trial is clearly and simply defined and easily recognized.

For each component of the discrete trial, there are important factors to remember that will enable an instructor to more successfully teach students with ASD.

Delivery of Instruction: Discriminative Stimulus

Delivery of the S^D (instruction) involves several critical steps. First, it should be presented in a simple, straightforward, and concise manner to ensure student understanding. Thus, for instance, a teacher's instruction to a student might be "Find circle" rather than "Can you find where the circle is?" This allows the student to hear only the two most important words—she is supposed to *find* something, and that something is a *circle*. Extraneous language can confuse the student or cause her to attend more to the other words or lose her attention altogether. Later, when attempting to help the student generalize her skills, the teacher should add more words to the instructional commands and statements.

Second, all instructors need to be consistent in the way they present the S^D, including how they present stimulus materials, the language they use, and so forth. This is especially important during the initial teaching phase of each skill. Later, as the student advances with his skills, instructors need to add words to the instructional phrase, add different instructional phrases and sentences, and otherwise present commands and directions in a fashion that is more typical of routine instruction.

Third, only when the student is paying attention and motivated to respond should the instructor provide an S^D. This step is an important and crucial part of the student's learning and is foundational for the success of future learning. If students fail to learn to attend to someone who is speaking to them, they will have significant difficulty acquiring skills. It is a skill that will be displayed differently by each student. It does not necessarily include maintaining eye contact with the instructor. Attending means that the student is ready to receive the S^D and is motivated to provide a response. A student shows that she is ready when she

- is not preoccupied with any other activity, object, or person and
- is stationary in the appropriate location designated by the instructor.

It is evident that a student is motivated when she indicates that she wants to obtain a specific reinforcer that the instructor has made available contingent on a correct response. Teachers must continuously evaluate the effect of the reinforcers they are using to find out what the student wants and, therefore, what will help motivate the student to respond to the S^D and acquire skills.

While it is most desirable for a student to attend by looking directly at the instructor when he is providing an S^D, that should not be initially expected or required due to the difficulty that students with ASD often display in acquiring that skill. It is not realistic to believe that, by forcing a student to look at the instructor's face or eyes, the student can be made to attend to the instructor. An instructor can help the student learn how to be ready for instruction by taking a known tangible reinforcer, bringing it up in front of his own face to direct the student's eyes toward his face, and simultaneously orienting the student toward the source of instruction and reinforcement. It also is beneficial for the first S^D of a session or series of trials to require an easy or already acquired response—something the student knows and will be successful with. Beginning a session on a successful note will often help to ensure that the student will attend to future S^Ds.

Fourth, the instructor should present an S^D only once. Only if it is apparent that the student did not hear the instructor, or was not attending, should the instructor provide the S^D again. If a student is accustomed to an instructor providing an instruction an indeterminate number of times, the student will learn that he may respond whenever he wants to. This can lead to difficulties with compliance with other instructors, as well as difficulty with learning appropriate social interaction skills. For example, if a typical peer has to ask the student a question more than two times, the peer may lose interest in pursuing further interaction. If the student learns that the instructor will provide the instruction only once and, if no response is provided, no reinforcement will be received (the instructor instead commences with the correction procedure, which will be discussed later), the student is more likely to learn to respond the first time an instruction is provided.

Fifth, the student's name should not be used within the S^D. It may seem beneficial to use a student's name (e.g., "Johnny, give me sock") because it is a way of obtaining the student's attention. Yet there are a couple of possible adverse effects that may hinder the student's future learning. First, by using a student's name, the instructor may inadvertently teach the student that she needs to pay attention only when her name is used in the

S^D. Therefore, even when she is the only one present with the instructor and the instructor says, "Give me sock," the student may not respond. Second, if a student hears her name within each S^D throughout the day, her name may become aversive. She may run away or purposely not attend to the instructor when she hears her name, because she has learned to associate an instruction with it.

 Quick Review: Delivery of Instruction
Present instruction
- in a *concise* manner,
- *consistently* across all instructors,
- only when student is *attending* and *motivated,*
- only *once,* and
- *without* using the student's name.

Obtaining the Correct Response

The second part of the DTT method, response (R), is composed of three elements that are connected to a student's ability to provide a correct response. First, it is important for all instructors to agree upon and consistently use correct response criteria. An example of two instructors accepting different responses follows:

- Instructor 1 says, "Where is your nose?" Student points in the general direction of his nose without actually touching it.
- Instructor 2 says, "Where is your nose?" Student actually touches his nose.

Adverse effects can result if different instructors accept different responses from a student as being correct. The student may become confused and give a different response to each instructor each time he is asked to respond to an S^D. Inconsistent standards may result in students learning different sets of skills for different instructors and responding in a certain way based on who is providing the S^D.

Second, instructors need to ensure that the response a student provides is not chained to another response. It is important that a student provide only one response to an S^D. When a student is unsure of what response to provide, she may attempt many different responses in the hope that one of them is correct. An example follows:

S^D: "Show me jumping."

R: Pats head, waves, jumps up and down.

If the instructor reinforces the student after she has provided the correct response along with other responses, the student may learn that all three behaviors are "jumping" and will then be confused when she is requested to "show waving" or "show patting head."

Third, the instructor needs to wait approximately 1 to 7 seconds after the S^D is delivered for the student to provide her response. It is important for the student to have enough time to recall the correct response, while also maintaining attention to the task at hand. The amount of delay time between the S^D and the response will vary for different students and skills. Accordingly, instructors need to collaborate to decide on an acceptable delay time. The following four components need to be considered in this decision:

1. *Difficulty of the task.* Typically, the more difficult the task, the longer the delay between the S^D and the response. Often, an instructor can see that a student is thinking and attempting to recall the correct response. As long as the student appears to be thinking or problem solving, the instructor should wait for the student.

2. *Fluency.* This refers to how quickly and accurately a student can provide a correct response. Fluency is not expected when a student is acquiring a new skill. Also, each time a new skill is introduced into the same category of acquired skills (e.g., within the "food" category, a student is provided novel food items in addition to the ones he already knows), it will affect the fluency of production of the already acquired skills.

3. *Determination of time needed to respond.* Some instructors use "rapid responding," wherein they require students to respond within 1 second after receiving an S^D; if a student does not do so, the instructor immediately prompts him to provide the correct response. Rapid responding may be appropriate for some students when working on fluency of acquired skills but not for skill acquisition. Adjustment of response time should be based on whether students are working on new skills or an acquired skill. After working with a particular student, instructors should be able to see a pattern in that student's learning habits. Based on that analysis, instructors should be able to accurately determine approximately how long they should wait for a response when teaching a new skill or attempting to generalize acquired skills.

4. *Avoidance of prompt dependency.* A student becomes prompt dependent when she consistently waits for an instructor's prompt before providing a correct response. Prompt dependency may result under the following conditions:

- Students with ASD may become upset when they fail at a task, so they figure out ways to ensure that they do not fail and look for any type of prompt, subtle or obvious, to point to the correct response.

- Instructors provide prompts that are not systematically faded quickly enough.
- Subtle prompts (which the instructor did not intend to provide) are consistently provided along with the S^D and not faded. For example, when asking a student to pick the red item in a display of green, blue, and red blocks, the instructor's eyes look at the red stimulus.
- Students with ASD are unmotivated to respond and learn that when they don't respond correctly (or don't respond at all), they are assisted in making the correct response.

It is imperative that instructors and those who supervise instructors of students with ASD have a carefully developed protocol related to the prompts and prompting methods that will be used. Prompting and fading methods are discussed later.

Quick Review: Obtaining the Correct Response
- Know the correct response expected.
- Ensure that the response is *not chained* to another response.
- When waiting (1–7 seconds) for the correct response, take into consideration the following:
  —difficulty of task
  —fluency
  —response time .
  —prompt dependency
  —acquisition of new skill vs. generalization of acquired skill

Providing Immediate Consequences

The third part of the DTT method involves consequences for students' responses. In this connection two matters are particularly important. First, an instructor needs to provide feedback (consequences) to the student after she provides a response to an S^D. Because students with ASD have difficulty learning, it is crucial that the instructor present the appropriate consequence immediately following the response. Here is an example of an instructor providing inappropriate feedback (consequences):

S^D: Instructor says, "Show me clapping."

R: Student claps her hands appropriately.

S^R: Instructor rummages through a box next to her looking for a specific toy to give to the student as a reinforcer for making

11

the correct response; several seconds later she hands the toy to the student and says, "Good clapping."

In the meantime, the student sat and watched another student play with a music toy and then looked out the window. When she finally receives the toy and hears "Good clapping," she may not remember that she just did clapping or may not pay attention to the "Good clapping" and think she got the toy for appropriate sitting. Providing *immediate* reinforcement for a correct response will increase the likelihood that the correct response will occur the next time the same S^D is provided. Here is an example of an instructor providing appropriate feedback (consequences):

S^D: Instructor says, "Show me clapping."

R: Student claps her hands appropriately.

S^R: Instructor immediately says, "Good clapping" and hands the student a ball.

Second, it is important for instructors not to *inadvertently* reinforce an incorrect response. Instructors may not realize that they are accepting a response as correct when other instructors are not accepting it. For instance, some instructors may say, "Good job" before they proceed with a correction procedure because they want to reinforce the student for trying to provide the correct response. By saying that, however, they may be communicating to a student that an incorrect response was correct. As previously indicated, some instructors may also reinforce a student for providing a correct response within a chain of other responses. It is essential that all instructors provide clear and consistent reinforcement and feedback. If a student provides an incorrect response, the instructor's immediate response should be to initiate a correction procedure that teaches the student the correct response. If a student's response is correct, the immediate result should be reinforcement that further strengthens the behavior.

 Quick Review: Providing Immediate Consequences
Remember to
- provide immediate reinforcement for a correct response, and to
- avoid inadvertent reinforcement of an incorrect response.

Summary

Using the discrete trial teaching method to teach students with ASD can be viewed as both complicated and simple. It can appear complicated because there are many steps to remember when using it to teach a student new skills. Yet, in reality, it is a simple and straightforward instructional method.

DTT primarily consists of three major components: (a) the instructor provides a simple instruction (S^D), (b) the student provides a response (R), and (c) the instructor provides a consequence to the student's response (S^R). The other considerations that have been discussed help instructors teach new skills and help students learn new skills within the framework of those three major elements. Once instructors start using the method, the steps will become automatic.

It is beneficial to spend time practicing the DTT method with co-workers before using it with children and youth with ASD. That ensures that practitioners are comfortable and consistent with the process and that they have an opportunity to provide feedback to one another and to sharpen their skills before using DTT with students. The table that follows can be used by teams of instructors to structure their practice. It includes columns for recording appropriate S^D phrases, correct student responses, and appropriate consequences.

S^D	R	S^R
Instructor says, "Give me pencil."	Student picks up and hands instructor the pencil.	Instructor says, "Great, Michael—this is pencil!"
Instructor holds up a child's book and says, "Where is the dog?"	Student points to the dog in the picture.	Instructor says, "Yeah! You found the dog! Good work!"
Instructor and student are standing in front of a sink and instructor says, "Wash your hands."	Student picks up the soap and starts playing with it.	Instructor takes soap, puts it back down, and says, "Let's try again."

Once instructors become adept with the basic skills involved in using DTT, they need to understand other crucial aspects of using DTT with students with ASD. The next section of this manual discusses those components, which will help instructors to provide the structure that students with ASD need to successfully learn and generalize new skills.

Providing a Structured Teaching Environment for Skill Acquisition

A structured teaching environment is vital to successfully using the DTT method. The following concepts, methods, and procedures are important for instructors to employ:

- errorless learning
- reinforcement
- pairing
- instructional control
- session management
- prompting and fading
- shaping
- correction procedure

Each of these teaching concepts, methods, and procedures is discussed individually within the following subsections. Each subsection contains the following:

- a definition (also provided in the glossary),
- a detailed explanation of the concept and implementation of the necessary procedures,
- examples of using the procedures with students with ASD,
- a "Practice Role-Play Scenario" for practicing the procedures, and
- a brief review of the important concepts regarding that procedure.

Observation forms to be used when the reader practices the procedures are provided in the appendixes.

Errorless Learning

Errorless learning involves teaching a new skill in a manner that minimizes the possibility of errors and thus increases the possibility that the student will be a successful learner. Errorless learning

- minimizes the number of errors a student will make,

- increases the time available to the instructor to engage in teaching rather than correcting the student,
- reduces the likelihood that errors will be repeated in the future, and
- reduces a student's frustration and inappropriate behaviors by increasing opportunities for the student to be reinforced for correct responses.

Everyone has memories of having difficulty learning a new skill. For all learners, including those with ASD, there are typically three reasons that people cannot successfully acquire a skill:

- they do not have the abilities required to perform the skill;
- they do not have the desire to learn the skill; or
- they are not appropriately taught how to perform the skill.

If instructors ensure that they are correctly and appropriately teaching skills to students with ASD, they can then concentrate on whether the student has the ability to acquire and perform the skill and is motivated to learn the skill. Thus, errorless learning is a teaching method in which an instructor ensures that she is assisting a student to successfully learn a skill if the student is motivated and capable.

A practical example of errorless learning can be found in sports. Athletes on a sports team routinely learn new skills and work to improve acquired skills. Their coaches are responsible for teaching them the skills they need to compete. When a new player joins a team, the coach typically does not expect that individual to already have all the skills she needs to compete and be a successful and proficient team member. When coaches teach their students a new skill, they must:

- ensure that the students are motivated to learn,
- break the skill into smaller steps,
- explain the function and use of the skill,
- demonstrate the skill,
- provide prompts needed to perform the skill initially,
- shape performance of the skill,
- provide immediate and relevant feedback regarding performance of the skill, and
- require that the students practice the new skill so that they become fluent in its execution and can use it at any appropriate time or place.

If coaches merely tell students to perform a skill that they have not yet acquired and have no prior knowledge of, the students will begin the learning process by making mistakes. Those mistakes may hinder the students from being successful in the future and increase their frustration, thereby decreasing their motivation to learn the skill. This same pattern applies to teaching students with ASD.

The two most important times during the DTT process to use errorless learning with a student are

- each time a new skill is taught, and
- when a student is demonstrating difficulty with an acquired skill.

An instructor needs to break each new skill into small, acquirable steps; model and otherwise demonstrate the skill; and then initially provide a high level of prompting, thereby ensuring motivation while decreasing frustration and increasing the likelihood that a student will be able to provide a correct response. This will increase the probability that the student will be successful in the future, as the instructor begins to fade the prompts. The process of fading will be discussed later in this book.

When a student is demonstrating difficulty with learning a new skill or is consistently demonstrating incorrect responses for a previously acquired skill, an instructor needs to immediately stop requiring independent responses. The instructor should begin a process of "backing up" in order to diagnose the learning difficulty and find out where the student is able to provide an independent successful response. Once this is achieved, the instructor employs the errorless learning approach and begins to proceed by breaking down a given skill into small steps, demonstrating the skill, and providing a high level of prompting when presenting the S^D. Providing a high level of prompting along with an S^D is an integral part of the errorless learning process. This allows the instructor to

- maintain the student's motivation, while decreasing his frustration, and
- increase the likelihood of future correct answers.

 Quick Review: Errorless Learning

Errorless learning helps an instructor to
- minimize the number of errors a student displays;
- reduce the likelihood that errors will be repeated;
- reduce the student's level of frustration and the occurrence of inappropriate behaviors;
- increase time available to teach; and
- increase opportunities for reinforcement of correct responses.

Remember to
- use this approach when teaching a new skill or helping a student who is having difficulty with an acquired task;

17

- present an S^D with enough of a prompt to ensure a correct answer; and
- provide a high level of reinforcement for a prompted correct response.

Reinforcement

The premise that a student needs to be motivated in order to learn is well documented. When using the DTT process, instructors employ reinforcement and prompting to motivate students to learn. Prompting will be explained in detail later. *Reinforcement* involves providing a consequence following a student's response that increases the likelihood that the response (behavior) will occur again in the future. A reinforcer is anything that the student wants to gain (e.g., food, attention, avoidance of difficult tasks). It is important to note that any behavior or response—inappropriate (incorrect) or appropriate (correct)—can be reinforced. It is, therefore, important for instructors to closely monitor the type of consequences that follow a student's responses. Four examples are provided to demonstrate appropriate use or withholding of reinforcement and inappropriate use or withholding of reinforcement. Some of these examples are similar to previous examples provided:

Reinforcement of Appropriate Behavior

A: Adult is holding a cookie within view of a child.

B: Child asks adult, "Cookie, please?"

C: Adult gives the child the cookie and says, "Good asking."

No Reinforcement of Inappropriate Behavior

A: Adult is holding a cookie within view of a child.

B: Child throws a tantrum and tries to take the cookie from the adult.

C: Adult ignores the child, walks away, and hides cookies.

Reinforcement of Inappropriate Behavior

A: Adult is holding a cookie within view of a child.

B: Child throws a tantrum and tries to take the cookie from the adult.

C: Adult gives the child the cookie.

No Reinforcement of Appropriate Behavior

A: Adult is holding a cookie within view of a child.

B: Child asks adult, "Cookie, please?"

C: Adult ignores the child and does not give the child the cookie.

The first and second examples illustrate an instructor who is *appropriately reinforcing* a student for a correct response and not reinforcing a student for an incorrect response. This instructor is appropriately using reinforcement to increase appropriate responses or behaviors and decrease inappropriate responses or behaviors. The third and fourth examples present an instructor who is *inappropriately reinforcing* a student for an incorrect response and not reinforcing a student for a correct response. This instructor is inappropriately using reinforcement and will likely increase inappropriate responses or behaviors and decrease appropriate responses or behaviors.

There are two primary purposes for using reinforcement during the DTT process. First, reinforcement is a critical factor in teaching a student new skills. By tying reinforcers directly to the target behavior that the instructor wishes to increase, the student is taught the correct response. Second, reinforcers can provide the motivation a student needs to learn a skill that he may not necessarily care about or whose importance he does not understand. A student needs to see a reason (a "payoff") for providing a response, specifically a correct response, to an S^D. If the instructor makes it clear that he has something the student wants to obtain, the student will be more apt to be motivated to do what the instructor requests in order to obtain that item or activity (the reinforcer).

It is imperative that instructors use reinforcers that the *student* prefers and not reinforcers that the *instructor* chooses and thinks the student prefers. Consistently employing the use of a reinforcer assessment (a checklist of items and activities the student has preferred in the past and novel, age-appropriate items the student may prefer) will allow an instructor to find out what the student wants to gain and will provide ideas for new items and activities that the student may like. Because the strength of a reinforcer (the amount of motivation that the reinforcer elicits) can vary from moment to moment, instructors need to implement a quick reinforcement survey at the beginning of each learning session. This will ensure that the student is highly motivated and decrease the likelihood of incorrect responses due to lack of motivation. When possible, it is appropriate and beneficial to allow the student to choose (prior to a learning session) what he would like to earn as a reinforcer after successfully completing a particular learning session (a larger reinforcer than what is earned at intervals during the learning session). Choice, in and of itself, can be a motivating factor that leads to successful learning, as it can make a student feel that he has some control over his environment and his learning. For example, an instructor knows that a particular student enjoys looking at books, playing on the computer, and playing with trains, so he pulls out a board with some pictures on it when he and the student sit down to begin working together. One picture shows a student working appropriately with an instructor, and there is an arrow to a blank spot. There are three pictures at the bottom of the board of the student reading books, playing on the computer, and playing with trains. The instructor asks the student to pick what activity he would like to do after "doing good work." The student picks a picture and puts it next to the arrow, establishing his choice to play with trains when they finish working. The board remains visible throughout the session.

There are three crucial factors that an instructor needs to take into consideration regarding the use of reinforcers. First, there should be reinforcers that the student has access to only during learning sessions and not during the rest of the day, either at home or at school. This ensures that the reinforcers maintain their strength and that the student does not become satiated. These items may be kept in special containers in locations that the student cannot access. Special reinforcers may also be used for some specific, very difficult learning activities. For example, if a student loves M&Ms and particularly dislikes writing activities, a teacher might provide one whole M&M to the student for every word she writes without protesting. Those candies would not be used during other learning sessions.

Second, the amount or level of reinforcement provided to the student needs to match the level of difficulty or desirability of the task he is being asked to perform. If the student enjoys the task or the task is fairly easy for the student, he requires smaller amounts of reinforcement or reinforcement at less frequent intervals. If the student dislikes the task or the task is difficult, he will likely need a larger amount of reinforcement or reinforcement at more frequent intervals. Instructors need to pay attention to the amount of motivation that the student displays to perform various tasks and provide only enough reinforcement to ensure that the student maintains a high enough level of motivation to perform a particular task. High motivation needs low reinforcement; low motivation needs high reinforcement.

Third, the student needs to be provided access to reinforcers *only* when she has earned them. That is, to receive a reinforcer, students must comply with a request or respond correctly to an instruction. Inappropriate behavior, noncompliance, and incorrect responses do not earn reinforcement. In order for the student to learn, she must understand that she must do or give something in exchange for something that she wants to gain.

If these DTT-related reinforcement skills are not learned and followed by instructors, their ability to teach students with ASD will be impeded. Thus, the process of a student learning a skill is the responsibility not only of the student but of the teacher, as well. If a student is not learning a particular skill, instructors need to analyze whether reinforcement is being appropriately employed. They must ask the following questions:

- Is the student being provided access to reinforcers as a consequence of making correct responses?
- Does the student want to gain the reinforcer that is being offered?
- Is the student being provided reinforcement only when he provides a correct answer?
- Does the amount of reinforcement match the difficulty or preference level of the task?

Practice Role-Play Scenario

Have two people work together as an instructor and a student, or have an instructor work with a real student with ASD. Pick a certain skill to work on while a third person observes and analyzes how the instructor reinforces the student during the session. Review together. Appendix A provides a reinforcement observation form.

Quick Review: Reinforcement

Remember to

- use items and activities that are highly preferred by the student as reinforcers;
- provide access to reinforcers only when the student has earned them and only in small amounts;
- allow access to specific reinforcers only during work sessions;
- see that the amount or level of reinforcement matches the level of difficulty or desirability of the task;
- consistently perform reinforcer assessments in order to keep a current record of the student's likes and dislikes; and
- gradually increase expectations of correct responses for the same level of reinforcement.

Pairing

Pairing is a process whereby the instructor establishes herself as a reinforcer by associating herself with other already existing reinforcers. She pairs herself with items and activities that the student already prefers and thus establishes herself as a reinforcer. She becomes a person the student wants to be with, rather than a person the student tries to get away from or is unmotivated to be near. Pairing is important because it establishes a foundation on which an instructor can build to teach students skills they need to learn. If students like to be with their instructors, they will be more motivated to do what is requested of them.

Most students with ASD will have a history of previously working with at least one instructor, and sometimes many. As a result, these students frequently have a presumption of what to expect from instructors, and their expectation may be good or bad, affecting their desire to learn positively or negatively. Establishing rapport with a student will directly affect an instructor's ability to teach and the student's willingness to learn. If appropriate pairing has correctly taken place, the student will be more apt to view the instructor as a "giver of good things," which would positively affect the student's learning.

There are two critical steps that an instructor uses to pair with a student. First, the instructor identifies items and activities that the student prefers and consistently seeks. The instructor then plays with those items with the student or engages in those activities with the student, as in the following examples:

- If the student likes to play with musical books, the instructor sits with the student and reads a book with him, and together they push the buttons to activate the music.
- If the student likes to swing, the instructor goes outside with the student and pushes him on a swing and talks and laughs with him.

Such sharing begins the pairing or bonding process. After several times of engaging in play with the student using such items and activities, the student will be more inclined to want to be with the instructor.

Second, as much as possible, instructors need to avoid associating themselves with negative events. For example, if a student has been playing alone with a preferred item or activity, an instructor should briefly play with the student in the presence of or using the preferred item or activity before transitioning her to a less preferred activity. This will ensure that the student does not associate the instructor with the removal of preferred items or activities.

The following are several reminders that are important for the instructor to do when pairing with a student:

- offer access to reinforcers that the student cannot access independently (can obtain only through the instructor);
- offer access to reinforcers in small amounts to increase the frequency of interaction with the student;
- gradually increase the demands placed on the student in order to gain the reinforcer; and
- pair frequently with the student, not just when first getting to know or starting to work with the student.

The following are reminders that are important for the instructor not to do when pairing with a student:

- do not interrupt the student while she is engaging in a reinforcing activity (unless it is time to end the activity);
- do not turn reinforcement into a task;
- do not place demands on the student when initially pairing with her; and
- if a student gains access to a reinforcer when she should not have it, do not attempt to grab it away; instead, distract the student and then discreetly remove it or ask for it (see discusson of give-it-back routine under "Instructional Control").

To maintain rapport with a student, an instructor needs to be mindful of pairing

- when first beginning to get to know and work with the student,
- at the beginning of every work session,
- throughout the work sessions, and
- outside of work times.

It is important for the instructor to make time to simply play with the student and not work. This allows the student to view the instructor as fun to be with independent of work.

An instructor must constantly evaluate herself to make sure she has appropriately paired with a student. One key factor to consider is whether the student runs *to* or *away from* the instructor. It is also important for the instructor to evaluate whether she looks forward to or avoids working with the student. Teaching should be just as enjoyable for the instructor as learning should be for the student.

Pairing with a student also presents an opportune time to conduct reinforcer assessments, in which the effectiveness and strength of reinforcers are evaluated frequently. During such times new items and activities can be introduced to the student to ascertain his interest in them. A record of those the student consistently likes and does not like can be maintained as a part of his record.

Practice Role-Play Scenario

Have two people play together as an instructor and a student, or have an instructor play with (or next to) a real student with ASD. A third person observes and analyzes how the instructor pairs with the student throughout the play session. Review together. Appendix B provides a pairing observation form.

Quick Review: Pairing
Remember to
- pair yourself with existing reinforcers to establish and maintain rapport with the student;
- avoid associating yourself with negative events; and
- reevaluate continually to make sure pairing is effective.

Instructional Control

Instructional control refers to the instructor creating a high probability of evoking a correct response. Establishing instructional control involves understanding the sequence of events that prepares a student to respond appropriately to and learn from an instructor. It also prepares the instructor to successfully teach the student. By pairing oneself with reinforcers that motivate the student to give correct responses, an instructor can establish a successful learning pattern for the student and thereby increase instructional control.

Thus, the two critical elements involved in establishing instructional control are the association of the instructor with the delivery of reinforcement (pairing) and having students provide correct responses subsequent to receiving the S^D. These elements are independent of one another, but if either one is not occurring, the instructor will be unable to establish instructional control.

Both of these elements relate to the instructor pairing process. Once an instructor and a student have successfully paired and the student views the instructor as a reinforcer, the instructor can establish student compliance with the instructions (S^D). The instructor gradually increases the demands placed on the student in order for the student to gain instructor reinforcement. Initially, every instruction provided by the instructor will be reinforced by the instructor, thus strengthening the likelihood that the student will comply with (provide a correct response to) the next instruction. At first, the instructor will want to provide easy requests and instructions for the student to follow so that the student's motivation to comply will be high when task difficulty is increased. Thus, as instructional control is being established, compliance is primarily being worked on. Gradually, as the strength of the instructional control is increased, the frequency of reinforcement is decreased and the difficulty of the tasks is increased.

One particular skill to be worked on during the process of establishing instructional control is having the student give an item to the instructor when it is requested or stop an activity when told to do so. The goal is to teach the student to believe "Every time I give something to the instructor, I will get it back soon" or "Every time I have to stop doing something, I will be able to do it again soon." The instructor is establishing a relationship that is based on trust—students give items to the instructor because they know that if they give them to the instructor right away, they will get them back. Therefore, even though a student may not want to give a preferred item to an instructor or stop a preferred activity, she will do it upon the instructor's request because there is the much more preferred payoff of getting the item back or being able to do the activity again. If there is an item or activity that the student consistently refuses to give back or stop doing, that item or activity will likely be an unsatisfactory reinforcer because it inhibits, rather than increases, a student's learning success.

During the times that an instructor is pairing with a student, they can engage in "give it back" or "stop and do it again" routines. Initially, instructors may engage in parallel play with toys or activities that are similar to those with which the student is playing. Playing next to the student will show the student that this particular adult is not threatening; his presence does not mean that preferred items will be taken away or preferred activities always have to stop. Once the student displays consistent acceptance with this routine, the instructor attempts to briefly, and at varying intervals, interact with the student by touching the item with which the student is playing and saying something about it or otherwise attempting to briefly become part of the activity in which the student is engaging. This routine also continues until the student displays tolerance.

Next, the instructor finds a moment when the student's hands are not on the item (or are not clutching the item), picks it up, does one brief action with it, and then either puts it back down or hands it to the student. That is, for a moment, the instructor interrupts the student's activity and then allows it to continue. This routine continues, and the intervals and lengths of interruption increase—but the interruptions occur because the instructor is becoming a part of the activity in which the student is engaged, not because he is making the student do work on a specific skill. The instructor can make up games with the student in which they take turns with the item or engage in the activity (the words "my turn" and "your turn" can be used). Once the student displays consistent tolerance for this type of playing, it is appropriate to begin requesting the item directly or asking the student to stop an activity ("Give me _____" or "Come here" or "Time to stop _____"). It is important that the instructor takes the item or has the student stop the activity for only a few seconds and then gives it back or lets the student immediately resume playing. This continues to show the student that she will be able to play with the preferred item or activity again. Eventually, the instructor uses this skill during work sessions, so that there is not a struggle or display of noncompliance when he asks the student to come to complete a work session.

As noted in the pairing discussion, it is important to *maintain* instructional control. Instructional control is established over time. Accordingly, instructors need to continue to work at instructional control so that compliance with requests and instructions is maintained. The following methods are useful for maintaining instructional control and are similar to those used in pairing:

- **Instructors must provide only small amounts of reinforcement;** this maintains the strength of the reinforcer, which in turn increases the possibility of obtaining a correct response to an S^D.
- **Instructors need to maintain control of the reinforcers;** access to reinforcement is only through the instructor. This increases the interactions the instructor will have with the student and, therefore, potentially increases positive interactions with students, which causes them to view instructors as reinforcers.
- **Instructors must avoid presenting S^Ds that compete with any existing reinforcement;** competing with a reinforcer for the student's attention decreases instructional control. If the student already has the reinforcement that she wants, she will not be motivated to attend to or comply with the instructor's request, thus decreasing instructional control. This is why it is important for the instructor to obtain compliance with a request for an item or for cessation of an activity in which the student is engaged.
- **Instructors need to increase the number and difficulty of tasks gradually over time;** more should eventually be required for the same amount of reinforcement. Increasing the difficulty of tasks leads to the student gaining the ability to function more independently and typically within her environment. Also, if a student is not consistently challenged, she will be less motivated to attend to instruction or provide correct responses.

Practice Role-Play Scenario

Have two people work together as an instructor and a student, or have an instructor work with a real student with ASD. Pick a certain skill to work on while a third person observes and analyzes how the instructor establishes and maintains instructional control with the student during the session. Review together. Appendix C provides an instructional control observation form.

Quick Review: Instructional Control

To establish instructional control,
- pair yourself with reinforcement that motivates the student;
- place the contingency of reinforcement on compliance to instruction;
- provide easy requests at first;
- decrease the frequency and level of reinforcement and increase the difficulty of task as instructional control is increased;

- establish trust by returning items taken or returning to activities that were stopped;
- maintain control of reinforcers;
- present instructions that do not compete with reinforcers; and
- increase the number and difficulty of tasks.

Session Management

Session management involves structuring the instruction and work time to maximize opportunities for student learning. Successful session management depends directly on the strength of the instructional control the instructor has established with the student. Instructors who are able to maintain appropriate instructional control are more apt to engage students in positive learning experiences. The following guidelines are offered to help instructors maximize the benefits of each instructional session:

- Establish a specific time for the session and do not vary it greatly.
- Make sure that all reinforcers and learning materials are accessible and ready.
- Minimize distractions as much as possible for both you and the student.
- Pay close attention to the positioning of students, materials, and yourself. The student needs to have a clear visual field of the materials (presented in front of him) and needs to be sitting or standing so that he is comfortable and able to reach the materials.
- Take into consideration any sensory issues, age appropriateness, and level of student ability related to the materials that are chosen. For example, a student who consistently places small, roughly textured items in his mouth should not be exposed to such items during training.
- Ensure that you are in an appropriate position to present materials to students and that you use an appropriate voice tone and volume for the student to hear and understand you when presenting an S^D.
- Ensure that the instructional and reinforcement times are balanced to maximize learning while maintaining student motivation. Initially, more time and energy are spent reinforcing the student's efforts and correct responses; gradually, more focus will be placed on obtaining correct responses to S^Ds.
- Focus on making learning positive and fun for the student.
- Engage in playing with reinforcers with the student at appropriate times during the session.

- Mix new and mastered skills throughout the session in order to maintain the student's success and motivation.
- Reinforce spontaneous, appropriate behavior. Make attempts to catch the little things the student does that are appropriate and that are precursors to more important and difficult skills and surprise him with reinforcement for those behaviors to increase the possibility that they reoccur. For example, if a student is walking down a school hallway and spontaneously points to a picture of a duck on the wall and says, "Duck," you should get very excited and praise the student and also point to the duck (even if students are supposed to be quiet as they walk down the hallway).
- Always end each session on a positive note by ending either after a time of play with the student or after the reinforcement of a correct response. This will leave a positive memory in the mind of both you and the student and increase the possibility that the next session will be a positive and fun experience.

 Practice Role-Play Scenario
Have two people work together as an instructor and a student, or have an instructor work with a real student with ASD. Pick a certain skill to work on while a third person observes and analyzes how the instructor manages the session. Review together. Appendix D provides a session management observation form.

Quick Review: Session Management
Successful session management
- enables the instructor to maximize learning;
- depends on the strength of instructional control established;
- engages the student in a positive learning experience;
- occurs in any environment or location, with any materials, and lasts any amount of time; and
- is maximized by employing the preceding guidelines.

Prompting and Fading

Prompting and fading are integral elements of the DTT process. Without prompting and the fading of prompts, a student will neither learn a skill nor be able to independently display the skill. A *prompt* is a stimulus, provided along with an S^D, which aids the student in making a correct response. *Fading* is the systematic withdrawal of prompts. In order to effectively teach new skills and amend incorrect responses, instructors need to use a variety of prompts and fade them when appropriate. As indicated, a prompt is used when (a) teaching a new response or skill and (b) correcting a student's incorrect response.

Prompting is one of the most difficult skills for an instructor to master. It often involves a split-second decision about what type of prompt to use or when to use a prompt to ensure a correct response without making a student prompt-dependent. It is recommended that whenever a new prompt is introduced, the instructor immediately begin to plan how it will be faded.

There are many different types of prompts that an instructor can choose to use in order to assist a student in learning a skill. A list of these prompts follows, with an example of each:

- *Full physical prompt.* The instructor physically manipulates a part of the student's body in order to assist her with *completing* a particular action.

  S^D: Instructor says, "Do this." Instructor demonstrates clapping by clapping his hands, then gently puts his hands around the student's wrists and picks up her arms and hands.

  R: Instructor makes the student's hands clap a couple of times.

  S^R: Instructor lets go of the student's wrists and says, "Good clapping, [student's name]."

- *Partial physical prompt.* The instructor physically manipulates a part of the student's body in order to assist her with *starting* an action.

  S^D: A pair of scissors and a piece of paper are sitting on the table in front of the student. Instructor says, "Cut the paper" and takes the student's hand and gently places the student's fingers in and around the scissor handles and then lets go.

  R: Student independently completes the action of cutting the paper.

  S^R: Instructor says, "Great cutting, [student's name]."

- *Imitative prompt.* The instructor physically demonstrates the action (the correct response) while the student watches.

  S^D: Instructor says, "Clap hands" and claps his own hands as student watches.

  R: Student claps her hands.

  S^R: Instructor says, "Yeah, good clapping."

29

- *Gestural prompt.* The instructor provides a physical cue to indicate the correct response.

   S^D: There are pictures of different animals on the table in front of the student and instructor. Instructor says, "Give me the dog" and points to the picture of the dog.

   R: Student picks up the picture of the dog and hands it to the instructor.

   S^R: Instructor says, "That's right. This is the dog."

- *Full echoic prompt.* The instructor verbalizes the *entire* correct response.

   S^D: The instructor holds up a picture of a book in front of the student. Instructor says, "What is it?" and then immediately says, "Book."

   R: Student says, "Book."

   S^R: Instructor says, "Good job. This is a book."

- *Partial echoic prompt.* The instructor verbalizes the *beginning* sound of the correct response.

   S^D: The instructor holds a picture of the student's mom in front of the student. Instructor says, "Who is it?" and then immediately says, "Mmmm."

   R: Student says, "Mommy."

   S^R: Instructor says, "Yes, that is Mommy. Good job, [student's name]."

- *Position prompt.* The instructor places the materials in certain positions (in relationship to the student) in order to increase the likelihood of the student locating the correct item.

   S^D: The instructor has placed a red shoe closer to the student than a yellow shoe and a green shoe. Instructor says, "Go get the red shoe."

   R: Student picks up the red shoe and hands it to the instructor.

   S^R: Instructor says, "Good job. You found the red shoe!"

- *Direct verbal prompt.* The instructor provides a verbal instruction to tell the student how to complete one step of a multistep task.

   S^D: Instructor says, "Go wash your hands" and then says, "First, go to the sink."

R: Student goes to the sink, turns on the water, and washes his hands with soap and water.

S^R: Instructor says, "Great job washing your hands, [student's name]."

- *Indirect verbal prompt.* The instructor states a question that leads the student to determine the correct response.

  S^D: Instructor says, "Go wash your hands" and then says, "What do you need to do first?"

  R: Student gets up and goes to the sink. He then turns on the water and washes his hands with soap and water.

  S^R: Instructor says, "Nice job washing your hands, [student's name]."

Deciding on the type of prompt to use will often depend on the type of response being sought. For instance, if a student is being asked to *say* something, the instructor will use a type of *echoic* prompt; if the student is being asked to *do* something, the instructor will use a type of *physical* prompt.

It is also important for an instructor to decide when to use the least-intrusive prompt and when to use the most-intrusive prompt. The least-intrusive prompt is the most subtle prompt from which the student will be able to give the correct response. This is used when (a) the instructor is attempting to fade prompts or (b) the student has already acquired the skill but just made an incorrect response. The most-intrusive prompt is the most obvious prompt from which the student will give a correct response. This is used when (a) initially teaching a new skill or (b) engaging the error-less learning approach. The following are examples of providing a most-intrusive prompt and a least-intrusive prompt:

Most-intrusive prompt

S^D: "Give me the red shoe." Instructor takes the student's hand and puts it on the red shoe.

R: Student picks up the red shoe and hands it to the instructor.

S^R: Instructor says, "Good job. You found the red shoe!"

Least-intrusive prompt

S^D: "Give me the red shoe." Instructor points to the red shoe.

R: Student picks up the red shoe and hands it to the instructor.

S^R: Instructor says, "Good job. You found the red shoe!"

As stated previously, fading prompts is extremely important. A careful plan needs to be established regarding how a student will be prompted and how the prompts will be faded. Fading prompts ensures that students will not become dependent on the instructor's assistance to complete a task or provide a correct response. The final goal is for students to be able to independently provide a correct response or complete a task within a naturally occurring situation in a typical environment. In the process of fading prompts, the instructor provides higher levels of reinforcement for each correct response that the student provides with less prompting; a less-prompted response receives more reinforcement than a more-prompted response. This will increase the student's motivation to provide better and more independent responses and guard against prompt dependency. Another method of decreasing prompt dependency is to use a variety of prompt styles (decreasing the predictability of certain prompts) with a student. This also makes the learning process more realistic for the student.

It is crucial for instructors to avoid providing inadvertent prompts—unintentionally helping students to make correct responses. Inadvertent prompts can be very subtle and sometimes indistinguishable to the instructor, but not to students. For example, as described previously, when giving the S^D "Give me the red one," an instructor may inadvertently direct her gaze toward the red item on the table. The student notices that the instructor does this every time she asks for something. As a result, the student learns to wait and watch where the instructor is looking before making a response. It is a good idea for every instructor to be periodically observed by another instructor for inadvertent prompting while working with a student.

It is important to remember that a prompt is part of the discrete trial and should be provided simultaneously with or immediately following the S^D. Furthermore, after a student has given an incorrect response, it is important to restate the original S^D, then provide the prompt, so that the response will be given under the control of the S^D and not the prompt.

 Practice Role-Play Scenario

Have two people work together as an instructor and a student, or have an instructor work with a real student with ASD. The instructor picks a skill that the student is currently working on but has not yet acquired. A third person observes and analyzes how the instructor prompts the student and fades the prompts throughout the session. Describe the prompts used. Review together. Appendix E provides a prompting and fading practice observation form.

Quick Review: Prompting and Fading
Remember to
- establish a careful plan for prompting and fading;
- ensure that the type of prompt used is dependent upon the type of response required by the student;

- use the least-intrusive prompt possible;
- begin to fade the prompt as soon as possible after introduction;
- make a final goal for the student to be independent of prompts;
- avoid inadvertent prompts;
- provide the prompt simultaneously or immediately following the S^D; and
- restate the original S^D with the prompt if the first response is incorrect.

Shaping

Shaping is developing a new behavior or skill by reinforcing closer and closer approximations of the desired behavior. It is often incorrectly confused with prompting. Shaping is used when the instructor wants to teach a behavior or skill that a student is not yet able to perform. By systematically requiring closer and closer approximations of the desired behavior, an instructor is able to systematically move—or shape—a learner's response in the direction of the behavior being sought. An example of when shaping *should* be used would be when an instructor wants to *teach* a student to say "cookie." By initially accepting the sound "kee" for "cookie," the instructor can systematically teach the student to make closer and closer approximations of the desired response. Shaping should *not* be used when an instructor wants a student to say "cookie" who has been previously observed to say it, but will not say it when given the S^D "Say *cookie*." Because the latter student is capable of making the sought response, a shaping process involving acceptance of less than the complete utterance would be unacceptable.

There are three steps in the shaping procedure:

- First, the instructor identifies the *final* correct response (the *terminal response*)—for example, the ability to say "cookie."
- Second, the instructor identifies a response to use as a starting point (a behavior the student has the ability to do)—for example, the response "kee."
- Third, the instructor identifies the steps from the starting point to the final correct response (successive approximations)—for example, (1) "kee," (2) "ooo," (3) "oookee," and (4) "coookeee." These steps may change depending on the student's progress, abilities, and so forth.

It is important to make sure that the steps are small enough that the student can be successful in quickly mastering each new approximation.

The crucial and most difficult part of shaping is requiring the next step in the line of successive instructional approximations. Before an instructor can require the next-closest approximation, he needs to observe the student actually performing that behavior (anywhere and at any time). If the student has never been seen doing what is required, the instructor does not know whether the student can actually do it. When the starting response is occurring reliably and is under the control of the S^D, it is time to introduce and require the next response approximation. When moving to the next response, less reinforcement for the initial response is given, and more reinforcement is provided for attempts and correct responses for the new target approximation. It is important that all instructors working with the student agree and move together to achieve each approximation step. Instructors should also make sure not to remain too long on any one step. Often, failure to achieve a step or to successfully move to the next step is because the next step is too difficult, the steps between required actions are too large for the student, the student is not motivated, or the instructor is providing insufficient reinforcement.

 Practice Beginning Exercise
Identify a new skill that a student you work with needs to learn or will soon be learning. Write out the terminal response, starting point, successive approximations, and prompts leading to the terminal response in the following list:
- Terminal response: _____
- Starting point response: _____
- Successive approximations (steps): _____
- Prompts: _____

Practice Role-Play Scenario
Have two people work together as an instructor and a student, or have an instructor work with a real student with ASD. The instructor picks a skill that the student needs to begin learning. A third person observes and analyzes how the instructor shapes the student's responses through reinforcement and increasing the difficulty level of the response. Describe and review together. Appendix F provides a shaping observation form.

Quick Review: Shaping
Instructor needs to
- identify the final correct response;
- identify a response to use as a starting point;
- identify the steps from the starting point to the final correct response;

- observe the student performing a behavior correctly before moving to the next approximation or response;
- ensure that all instructors are working on the same tasks; and
- move along as quickly as possible.

When determining a succession of steps for shaping a target behavior, it is beneficial to consult with appropriate professionals to ensure step suitability. For example, for verbal responses consult with a speech–language pathologist to ensure developmental appropriateness when selecting successive steps.

Correction Procedure

A correction procedure is a consequence for an incorrect response or failure to respond following the presentation of an S^D. The correction procedure is a component of errorless learning; it strengthens the connection between the S^D and the response by increasing the likelihood that the response will be correct. It involves using prompts and fading prompts to obtain the correct response. Instead of saying "no" when a student provides an incorrect response and moving on to another trial, the instructor uses the opportunity to engage the errorless learning approach and teach the correct response. The goal of the correction procedure is to obtain the correct response under the control of an unprompted S^D. It is important to remember that this procedure is used only with skills that the student has acquired; it is not used when teaching a new skill.

This procedure is the most difficult to learn when using the DTT process and the most difficult to use when teaching a student a specific skill. As such, instructors need to practice this skill many times and continue to practice it until it becomes an automatic component of the DTT process.

Implementing the correction procedure begins once an incorrect response has been provided by the student and involves the following five steps:

Step 1. The instructor restates the original S^D.
- If the student now provides a *correct* response, the student is reinforced appropriately and the procedure ends.
- If the response is *incorrect*, the instructor and student continue to Step 2.
- If there is *no response*, the instructor must make sure she has the student's attention and then state the original S^D a second time. If the student provides a correct response, it is reinforced appropriately and the procedure ends. If there is still no response or

an incorrect response, the instructor and student continue to Step 2.

Step 2. The instructor adjusts the prompt level until the student successfully provides a correct response. The instructor repeats the S^D and provides the least-intrusive prompt.
- If the student provides a *correct* response, the instructor reinforces the student appropriately (but not with the highest level of reinforcement) and then proceeds backward (fading the prompts) by steps to the last unprompted S^D.
- If the student provides an *incorrect* response with this prompt, the S^D is repeated and a prompt is provided that is slightly stronger than the previous prompt.
- If there is *no response*, the instructor follows the same procedure as if the response was incorrect.

Step 3. The instructor presents the original, unprompted S^D. Depending on the student and the level and number of prompts provided to acquire the correct response in Step 2, the instructor will typically use a discrete trial to fade each prompt before providing the original S^D without any prompts.
- When the instructor finally provides the original S^D without any prompts and the student provides a *correct* response, the instructor needs to provide a high level of reinforcement, including praise.
- If the instructor provides the unprompted S^D and the student provides *no response* or an *incorrect* response, the instructor must return to Step 2 and work back to the previous unprompted S^D in order to obtain a correct response.

Step 4. The instructor provides a "distracter" trial. This is a trial that involves requesting the student to perform an easy and already acquired skill before once again returning to the target skill. The instructor provides the S^D for the distracter trial, obtains the correct response, and then provides a low level of reinforcement (matching the easy level of the response being required).

Step 5. The instructor once again provides the original unprompted S^D for the target skill. If the instructor obtains a correct response, a high level of reinforcement is provided to the student. This trial ensures that the student can still provide the correct response to the unprompted S^D subsequent to a period of time and a distraction following the last S^D presentation. Later in the work session it is also beneficial to again provide this S^D to make sure the student is still able to provide a correct response.

It is also recommended that instructors use the following techniques during the correction procedure:

- Before presenting an S^D, make sure that the student is attending and motivated and that the appropriate reinforcers are readily available.
- Restate the S^D before each new prompt is provided, so that the correct response is connected to and under the control of the S^D and not the prompt (to prevent the student from becoming prompt dependent).
- Reinforce every correct response. Regardless of the level of prompt provided, reinforcement must be provided for each correct response so that the student's efforts are acknowledged and she remains motivated to continue responding.
- Provide less reinforcement for any prompted responses.
- Save the most powerful reinforcer for the correct, unprompted responses, especially the correct response after the distracter trial.

If responses are not proceeding well with the correction procedure, the instructor may need to end the session on the most independent response and evaluate the session. When attempting to determine the difficulty, instructors are encouraged to consider varying the

- level of prompting,
- type of prompts,
- type and strength of reinforcer, and
- task being required of the student (e.g., its level of difficulty).

Practice Role-Play Scenario

Have two people work together as an instructor and a student, or have an instructor work with a real student with ASD. Pick a skill that the student has almost acquired. Practice using the correction procedure for incorrect responses made by the student. A third person observes and analyzes how the instructor implements the correction procedure. Describe and discuss together. Appendix G provides a correction procedure observation form.

Quick Review: Correction Procedure

Remember to
- use only with skills that the student has already acquired;
- use the five-step process:
  —restate the original S^D and go to Step 2 only if no response or an incorrect response is made

—adjust the prompt level until the student provides the correct response

—present the original unprompted S^D and obtain a correct response

—provide a "distracter" trial

—provide the original unprompted S^D again and obtain a correct response

- ensure that the student is attending and motivated;
- restate the S^D before each new prompt;
- reinforce every correct response; and
- save the most powerful reinforcer for correct, unprompted responses.

Figure 1 provides a diagram of the correction procedure, including the steps and the decision-making process that instructors are advised to follow.

What To Teach

To establish an appropriate teaching program for a student with ASD, the individuals or teams of professionals and parents will need to

- conduct a comprehensive skills assessment,
- develop a profile of the student's abilities and deficits,
- write a set of goals and objectives (e.g., an Individualized Education Program, or IEP) that addresses the student's deficits (after determining the specific skills to address),
- decide on and implement an education program to teach the new skills to the student, and
- use an appropriate data collection system for evaluating the student's progress.

Because individuals with ASD often demonstrate splinter skills (high levels of ability in some areas and inconsistent or low ability levels in others), a comprehensive skills assessment allows the curriculum planning team to gain a clearer picture of what "holes" they need to address. Once the assessment is complete, a thorough profile of the student's skills can be developed, thus displaying to the team what critical skills the student needs to learn.

Taylor and McDonough (1996) outlined five questions that should be kept in mind when assessing a child's skills: (a) "Is the skill demonstrated upon your verbal instruction?" (b) "Is the skill demonstrated without your

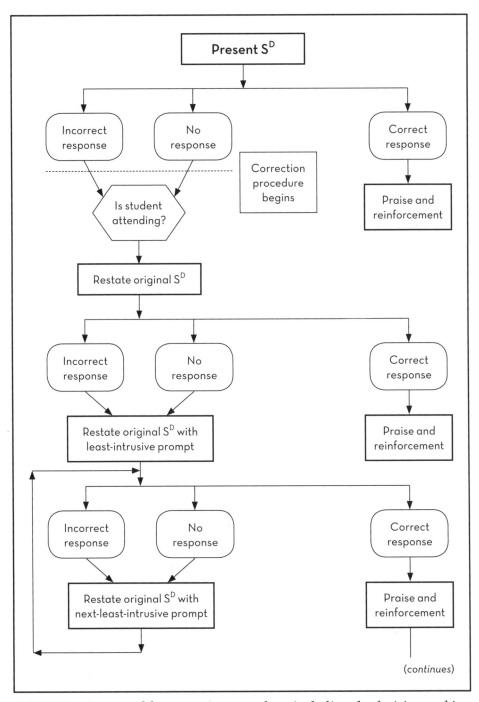

FIGURE 1. Diagram of the correction procedure, including the decision-making process.

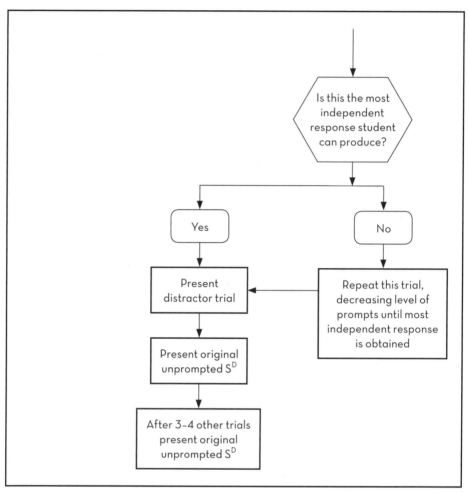

FIGURE 1. *Continued.*

assistance?" (c) "Is the skill demonstrated reliably over time?" (d) "Are all components of the skill demonstrated?" and (e) "Is the skill demonstrated with several different people, in several different contexts, with various stimuli?" (p. 63). Each of these questions is addressed in *The Assessment of Basic Language and Learning Skills: An Assessment, Curriculum Guide, and Skills Tracking System for Children with Autism or Other Developmental Disabilities* (ABLLS; Partington & Sundberg, 1998a). This is a criterion-referenced assessment tool designed to assess a child's current skills; it also provides educators and parents with a curriculum that assists in identifying educational objectives. This tool assesses a variety of language skills and accounts for the child's motivation to respond, ability to attend to a variety of stimuli (nonverbal and verbal), ability to generalize skills, and tendency to spontaneously use those skills (Partington & Sunberg, 1998a). The tool is divided into four sections of skills: (a) basic learner skills assessment (15 different skill sets, including cooperation and reinforcement effectiveness, receptive language, and social interaction); (b) academic skills assessment (4 different skill sets, including reading, math, and writing); (c) self-help skills assessment (4 different skill sets, including dressing, eating, and toileting); and (d) motor skills assessment (gross-motor and fine-motor skills).

Once an assessment of skills has been completed, ABLLS provides a set of profile grids to allow the IEP team to transfer the scores from the assessment to the corresponding grids for each skill and gain a summary or overall picture of the student's strengths and weaknesses. After the grids have been completed, the IEP team can determine appropriate goals and objectives that address the skill deficit areas that appear to be most critical. ABLLS provides corresponding goals and objectives that the team can use for each skill that is assessed.

Once the goals and objectives have been approved by the planning team, the next step is to design and implement an educational program that best meets the critical needs of the child. Questions that can be asked to help a team locate and determine an appropriate educational program are as follows:

- Does the child need certain prerequisite skills for this program?
- Is this program developmentally and age-appropriate for this child?
- Will this program help the child reduce problem behaviors and increase appropriate behaviors?
- Will this program allow us to address the critical skill deficits of this child?
- Will this program allow us to build on the strengths of this child?
- Does this program allow for skill generalization?
- Does this program allow the child to acquire skills within a reasonable amount of time?
- Does this program use a reliable data collection system to track the progress of the child's learning?

These questions need to be asked even when a team is thinking of using the DTT method with a child. DTT is not necessarily the only appropriate method of intervention for a child with ASD, and although it is appropriate for many, other intervention methods may also be needed to address some of the critical skill areas.

Once team members have decided upon an appropriate teaching program for a child with ASD, they will need to ensure that the instructors are (a) fully trained in the method of intervention and use of the appropriate curriculum and (b) able to use appropriate data collection methods to track the skills (acquisition and progress) of the child. This manual can be used to ensure that instructors are appropriately trained in the DTT method. Many resources are available to guide IEP team members and instructors in choosing an appropriate curriculum for the DTT they are developing, including *A Work in Progress: Behavior Management Strategies and a Curriculum for Intensive Behavioral Treatment of Autism* (Leaf & McEachin, 1999); *Behavioral Intervention for Young Children with Autism: A Manual for Parents and Professionals* (Maurice, Green, & Luce, 1996); and *Teaching Language to Children with Autism or Other Developmental Disabilities* (Partington & Sunberg, 1998b).

Data-Based Decision Making

Reliable and ongoing DTT data collection is essential for making effective decisions regarding a student's educational program. Indeed, having a data-based decision-making process to analyze and change students' programs and assist IEP teams in ensuring that students are receiving an individualized and appropriate educational program is mandatory. No two students respond in the same manner to a DTT program, and, therefore, only through data collection, analysis, and interpretation can an instructor and an IEP team understand a student's learning process. A brief and basic explanation of the purpose of data collection, types of data, selection and creation of data sheets, summerizing data, data analysis and interpretation, and using data to make decisions is provided in this section.

Purpose of Data Collection

Data collection needs to be used in all areas of a student's education program. It is recommended that a data collection system meet the following criteria for the skills and behaviors to be measured:

- It should be specific; it clearly defines the behaviors or skills to be measured.
- It should be valid; it actually measures what it claims to measure.
- It should be reliable; it remains consistent across observers.

If these three criteria are achieved, an IEP team will be able to use the data successfully for the following purposes:

- to understand how a student is progressing with each skill;
- to communicate to others at what level a student is performing;
- to demonstrate a student's mastery, generalization, and maintenance of skills;
- to improve the instructor's ability to provide optimal instruction; and
- to continue to provide an appropriate educational program.

Types of Data

The type of data collected will depend on the type of information that is needed to monitor progress and inform changes within a student's educational program. An IEP team or instructor will collect data that informs them about how a student is learning a particular skill. For example, if the intent of the program is to teach the student to "initiate conversation," it would be beneficial to know how many times in a play session that pupil initiates a conversation (rate data) and possibly how long each conversation lasts (duration data).

The following types of data are most frequently used when working with students with ASD to acquire, maintain, and generalize skills:

• *Accuracy data.* Data are collected to keep a record of a student's correct responses. These types of data (e.g., number of colors matched correctly out of 10 opportunities) are useful for teaching discrete skills, when skills are matched with opportunities to respond.

• *Proficiency or rate data.* Data are collected to record how often, in a given amount of time, the student performs a behavior. These data are useful for skills that occur at a low rate or during a specified time period (e.g., student initiated conversation seven times in a 20-minute free-play session).

• *Duration data.* These data measure how long a behavior lasts. They are useful for documenting challenging behavior (e.g., tantrums) and skills that need to last for a certain amount of time to be considered functional (e.g., student independently engaged with art materials for 5 minutes).

• *Latency data.* Latency data measure the length of time between the presentation of an instruction and the performance of the behavior or initiation of the behavior sequence (e.g., an instructor says, "Get your pencil" and then records the length of time that passes before the student retrieves his pencil).

• *Level-of-assistance data.* These data reflect how much help or what type of prompting a student requires to perform a behavior or task. These are useful for chained tasks that cannot be described as correct or incorrect (e.g., student required partial physical prompt to begin to follow direction "Put it on the shelf," direct verbal prompt to turn on the water to begin a hand-washing routine, and a gestural prompt to use the soap).

• *Work sample data.* These data are products of a student's performance related to a target skill. Work samples (e.g., a videotape of social interaction, a photograph of a block tower built by a student, a copy of a drawing) provide a snapshot of current progress and are useful for skills that are difficult to capture with a checklist or data sheet.

• *First trial data.* These data allow instructors to record only the first response of the student when given a specific S^D. They are useful when attempting to determine the independence of responding and mastery and the generalization of skills, and when working with more than one student at a time. For example, after analysis of every accuracy data trial, the instructor notices that, even though a student has 80% accuracy, many of his first responses are incorrect. Thus, the instructor questions whether the student has actually learned and maintained the correct response. Accordingly, first trial data are taken.

Selection and Creation of Data Sheets

There are many published and available data sheets suitable for use in DTT programs. However, because each student's program is individualized, data sheets will often need to be created to measure student progress on specific programs. Whether selecting an existing form or creating a new one, instructors are advised to address the following questions regarding the specific program and the skill or task being taught. Answers to these questions will assist in identifying the type of data sheet needed:

- Is the emphasis of the program on teaching a new skill or changing how the current one is being taught? *Example:* Is the team just starting to teach colors, or have they discovered that they need to change the method they were using to teach colors?
- What type of data will answer posed questions? The type of data collected will greatly narrow the type of data sheets that should or can be used. *Example:* Does the team need to take data that are + (occurrence) or − (no occurrence), or are they making tally marks on the occurrence of a behavior during a specified period of time?
- Will this type of data help address the IEP objective related to a particular skill? Instructors need to match closely the type of data collected to the language and skill of the objective to make sure that the information gained from the data sheet will enable changes to be made that will produce progress toward achieving the objective. *Example:* If a student is working on a goal to identify numbers 1 through 10, the IEP team will want to take data that allows them to know what percentage of the time that the student sees a 1, he correctly identifies it as 1; *and* if he is receptively or expressively identifing 1; *and* with how many other numbers presented in the display.
- Will this data collection format fit into the classroom activities? Instructors need to make sure that the data collection sheets are organized so that they are understandable to paraprofessionals, instructional assistants, and other instructors and will, therefore, be easy to read and use while interacting with and teaching the students. Instructors need to take the time to share and discuss the data sheets with the student's instructional team

45

before beginning to use them. *Example:* If it is a busy classroom with more than a 1:1 adult-to-student ratio, the data sheets need to be simple, with large spaces and lettering, and designed to take the instructor only a second to write down a data point in the correct location.

• How will the data be summarized? The design of the data sheet and the type of data should make it easy to follow the progress of the student; it should be well organized, with appropriate sections for information at a glance. *Example:* Because most data will ultimately be summarized in a graph, a data sheet needs to have the student's name, the skill being taught, the date of each time data was taken, and a field for the data points.

• How will the data be analyzed? Before too much data are taken with a new data sheet, it should be tested to see how the data will be summarized and analyzed. *Example:* Once data have been collected for a couple of days on a given skill, the classroom teacher should graph the data and see if she is able to analyze the data and determine some pattern of learning that is occurring; if not, she may need to pick a different type of data to use for that skill.

Each data sheet designed to measure a specific skill should have an accompanying program sheet that

- explains the procedures to be used for teaching each step of the new skill,
- provides an example of the type of data to use with the data sheet, and
- explains what mastery of the target skill will look like.

Figures 2, 3, and 4 provide examples of data sheets.

Summarizing Data

Summarizing data is a crucial part of determining the success of a student's DTT program. It is through the summary of data that an instructor and an IEP team will be able to locate patterns and determine whether suitable progress is being made. The goal of summarizing data is to display the progress a student is making in learning a specific skill, as well as to determine the student's unique learning patterns.

The manner in which data are summarized will depend on the type of data collected. Graphing is one of the most efficient and comprehensive ways to summarize and display data; it is suitable for the following types of data: accuracy, level of assistance, rate, duration, and first trial. Figure 5 provides examples of accuracy, rate, and duration data graphs.

Student: _____

Skill: _____

S^D: _____

+ = Correct   − = Incorrect   0 = No Response   P = Prompted   G = Generalization

Date	1	2	3	4	5	6	7	8	9	10	11	12	13	14	Total correct	Percentage	Initials

FIGURE 2. Generic data collection sheet.

Student: _____ Activity: _____

Date	Number of independent responses	Number of different materials independent	Number of prompts	Comments and Ideas

FIGURE 3. Example data sheet for student's appropriate use of materials during activity.

Date	Toy	Number of prompts	Length of play	Comments

Student: _____   Location: _____

FIGURE 4. Example data sheet for recording student's appropriate play.

Data Analysis and Interpretation

By studying a graph, an instructor can answer the question of whether the instructional procedures are working and determine whether the student is progressing and what patterns of learning are occurring. The goal is to provide the best instruction by eliminating ineffective teaching and interventions and implementing methods that prove to be effective. Summarizing and analyzing data need to occur frequently in order to make necessary instructional changes as early as possible.

The key component of data analysis is determining, not only whether a student is progressing, but also whether specific patterns are occurring that are assisting the student in or impeding him from learning new skills. In addition, it is important to understand the problem-solving process that data analysis and interpretation involve. Typically, there is no single reason for the results that the data display. The instructor will use the data to help the team determine a course of action with the understanding that they are engaging in hypothesis testing (e.g., "We believe that the data suggest that John is not learning [skill] because [reason]; therefore, we will now try to do [new procedures]"). If that plan works, the hypothesis was correct; if it did not, another hypothesis will need to be developed and another course of action taken.

Practice Data Analysis and Interpretation

Refer to the graphs in Figure 6 and attempt to determine (a) whether the student is progressing, (b) what might be impeding or assisting acquisition of the skill, and (c) what suggestions you might give the IEP team and instructor regarding future work on this skill. This exercise will be most

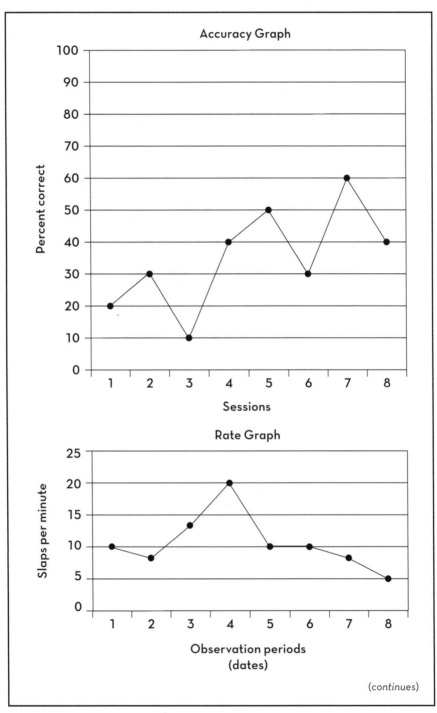

(continues)

FIGURE 5. Examples of accuracy, rate, and duration data graphs.

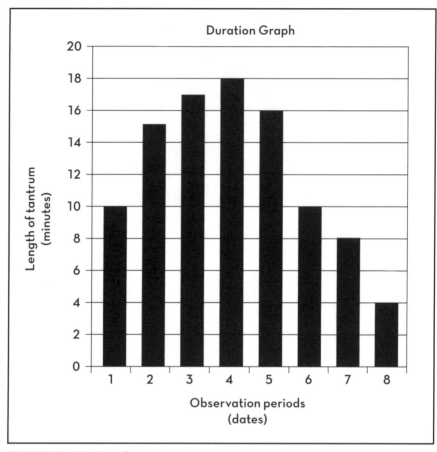

FIGURE 5. *Continued.*

beneficial if you attempt to analyze the data independently before reading the suggestions provided below each graph.

Using Data To Make Decisions

The diagram in Figure 7 provides an overview of the cyclical process of using data to assess and plan a student's educational program. Viewing that process as a cyclical routine enables one to understand how a team continually uses data to adjust and improve instruction in order to amend and improve each student's learning and progress.

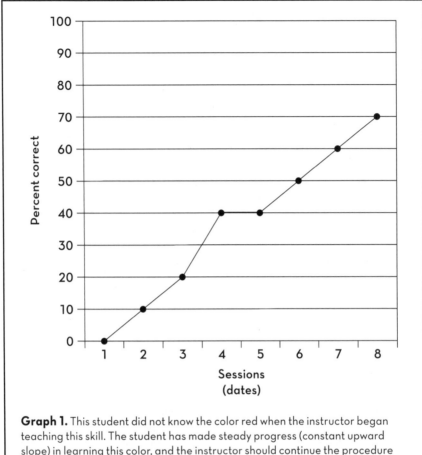

Graph 1. This student did not know the color red when the instructor began teaching this skill. The student has made steady progress (constant upward slope) in learning this color, and the instructor should continue the procedure that she is using to teach the skill. It is reasonable to expect the student to acquire this skill soon at ~ 100% accuracy.

(continues)

FIGURE 6. Sample graphs and analyses for data interpretation.

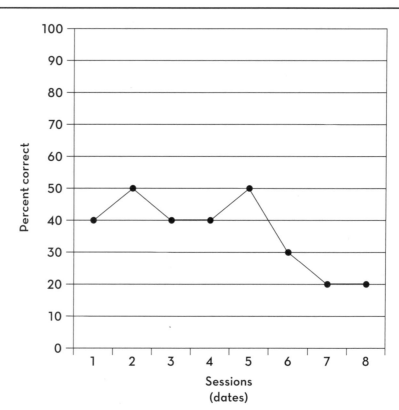

Graph 2. This student was able to identify the color red some of the time when the instructor began teaching this skill. For a while, the student maintained approximately the same level of ability (no downward or upward slope), and then he began to steadily lose the skill of identifying red (constant downward slope). The instructor should not continue using the procedure that he is using to teach the skill. It is reasonable to expect that if the instructor does not change the teaching procedure, the student will completely lose the ability to identify red and may have difficulty learning to identify colors in the future. Possible reasons for this loss of skill: (a) instructor does not have appropriate instructional control, (b) instructor is not providing appropriate reinforcement when the student does provide the correct answer, (c) the instructor is not providing enough or the right type of prompt to teach the student what "red" is, (d) the instructor is not ensuring that the student is attending before providing instruction, (e) the instructor is not using the correction procedure when the student provides an incorrect response, or (f) it is not the appropriate time to be teaching this skill.

(continues)

FIGURE 6. *Continued.*

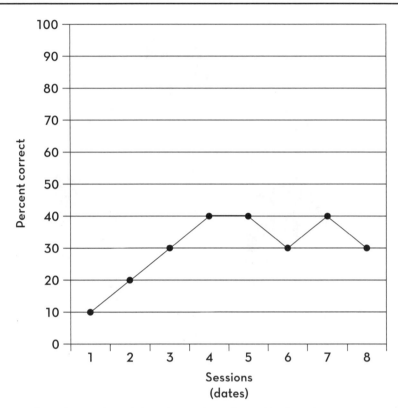

Graph 3. This student did not know the color red before the instructor began teaching this skill. The student began by learning the color red at a steady rate (constant upward slope). After a few sessions the student's learning plateaued (no downward or upward trend), and she has not made anymore progress. The instructor needs to reevaluate the teaching procedure and compare the data from the first four sessions to the data from the last four sessions to determine what changed and has impeded the student from progressing further. Once the impediment has been identified, the instructor needs to make appropriate adjustments to the teaching procedure before proceeding. To detect the impediment the instructor could examine (a) a change in instructors, (b) a change in type or level of prompting, (c) a change in type or level of reinforcement, (d) a change in materials used, (e) a change in the environment in which the student is taught, (f) a change in the student's personal life, and (g) and overall change in the student's learning progress across all skills, among other things.

FIGURE 6. *Continued.*

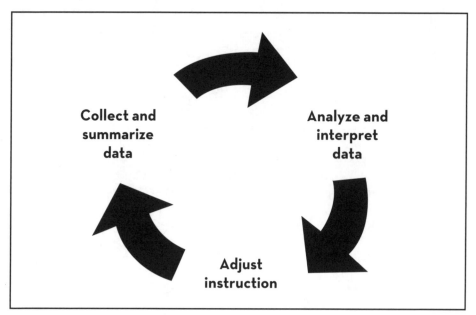

FIGURE 7. Data-based decision-making process.

The DTT instructional method can best be summarized as relying on the foundational S^D—R—S^R elements. These components, shown in Figure 8, provide an overall picture of how instructors may appropriately view DTT and at which point they will be implementing the various components of DTT as they teach students with ASD. It is important to note that

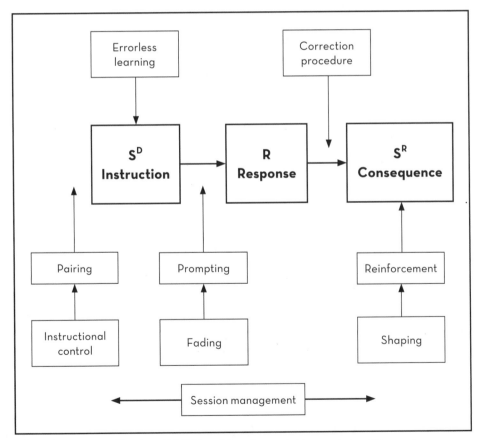

FIGURE 8. Overall veiw of DTT and implementation points of its various components.

while each of these skills is indicated as occurring at a different point during the DTT process, all of them involve using appropriate reinforcement in order to ultimately be successful.

DTT is a scientifically researched method that has been shown to produce positive results for children and youth with ASD (Lovaas, 1987; McEachin, Smith, & Lovaas, 1993; Smith, 2001). The DTT method provides teachers and others with a structured yet flexible and versatile tool for instruction of students with ASD. An instructor can use it within a 1:1 setting in a home or school environment; within a group setting; and for myriad purposes. DTT will not cure children and youth who have ASD, but it is an appropriate and effective method of teaching them and helping them to acquire the skills they need to function appropriately and independently within home, school, and community settings.

Antecedent: the stimulus under which a behavior occurs.

Applied behavior analysis: the process of systematically applying the principles of behavior in order to "improve socially significant behavior to a meaningful degree and to demonstrate experimentally" that the procedures used were actually responsible for the change (improvement) in the behavior (Cooper et al., 1987, p. 14).

Behavior: an action that occurs in response to an antecedent.

Chaining: the display of several responses in quick succession in the hope that one of them is correct.

Consequence: a response that follows a behavior that will either increase or decrease that behavior.

Correction procedure: a consequence for an incorrect response or failure to respond following the presentation of an S^D.

Discriminative stimulus (S^D): the instruction, question, or relevant materials presented to the student.

Errorless learning: teaching a new skill in a way that minimizes the possibility of errors and thus increases the possibility that the student will be a successful learner.

Fading: the systematic withdrawal of prompts that have been provided to help a learner correctly respond to an S^D.

Instructional control: the instructor's establishment of a high probability of evoking a correct response from a particular student.

Pairing: the instructor's linking of himself with items and activities that the student already prefers and thereby establishing himself as a reinforcer.

Prompting: a stimulus, provided along with an S^D, that aids the student in making a correct response. There are two ways of providing prompts:

- Least-intrusive prompt: the most subtle prompt from which the student will be able to give the correct response.
- Most-intrusive prompt: the most obvious prompt from which the student will give a correct response.

Rapid responding: the requirement of a student to respond within 1 second of receiving an S^D; otherwise, the instructor immediately prompts the student to provide the correct response.

Reinforcement: a consequence that follows a student's response and increases the likelihood that the response (behavior) will occur again in the future.

Reinforcer: something that the student wants to gain (e.g., food, attention, avoidance of difficult tasks).

Session management: structuring of instruction and work time to maximize opportunities for student learning.

Shaping: developing a new behavior or skill through reinforcement of closer and closer approximations of the desired behavior.

Strength of reinforcer: the amount of motivation that a reinforcer elicits.

References

American Psychiatric Association. (2000). *Diagnostic and statistical manual of mental disorders* (4th ed., text rev.). Washington, DC: Author.

Atwood, T. (1998). *Asperger's syndrome: A guide for parents and professionals*. Philadelphia: Kingsley.

Burack, J. A., & Volkmar, F. R. (1992). Development of low- and high-functioning autistic children. *Journal of Child Psychology and Psychiatry, 33,* 607–616.

Committee on Educational Interventions for Children with Autism: Division of Behavioral and Social Sciences and Education, National Research Council. (2001). *Educating children with autism*. Washington, DC: National Academy Press.

Cooper, J. O., Heron, T. E., & Heward, W. L. (1987). *Applied behavior analysis*. Upper Saddle River, NJ: Prentice Hall.

Green, G. (1996). Evaluating claims about treatments for autism. In C. Maurice, G. Green, & S. C. Luce (Eds.), *Behavioral intervention for young children with autism: A manual for parents and professionals* (pp. 15–43). Austin, TX: PRO-ED.

Koegel, R. L., Koegel, L. K., Frea, W. D., & Smith, A. E. (1995). Emerging intervention for children with autism: Longitudinal and lifestyles implications. In R. L. Koegel & L. K. Koegel (Eds.), *Teaching children with autism: Strategies for initiating positive interactions and improving learning opportunities* (pp. 1–15). Baltimore: Brookes.

Leaf, R., & McEachin, J. J. (Eds.). (1999). *A work in progress: Behavior management strategies and a curriculum for intensive behavioral treatment of autism*. New York: DRL Books.

Lovaas, O. I. (1987). Behavioral treatment and normal educational and intellectual functioning in young autistic children. *Journal of Consulting and Clinical Psychology, 55*(1), 3–9.

Mauk, J. E., Reber, M., & Batshaw, M. L. (1997). Autism and other pervasive developmental disorders. In M. L. Batshaw (Ed.), *Children with disabilities* (4th ed.). Baltimore: Brookes.

Maurice, C., Green, G., & Luce, S. C. (Eds.). (1996). *Behavioral intervention for young children with autism: A manual for parents and professionals*. Austin, TX: PRO-ED.

McEachin, J. J., Smith, T., & Lovaas, O. I. (1993). Long-term outcome for children with autism who received early intensive behavioral treatment. *American Journal on Mental Retardation, 97,* 359–372.

Myles, B. S., & Simpson, R. L. (2003). *Asperger syndrome: A guide for educators and parents* (2nd ed.). Austin, TX: PRO-ED.

Partington, J. W., & Sunberg, M. L. (1998a). *The assessment of basic language and learning skills: An assessment, curriculum guide, and skills tracking system for children with autism or other developmental disabilities* (2.1 ed.). Danville, CA: Behavior Analysts.

Partington, J. W., & Sunberg, M. L. (1998b). *Teaching language to children with autism or other developmental disabilities.* (7th ed.). Danville, CA: Behavior Analysts.

Simpson, R. L., de Boer-Ott, S. R., Griswold, D. E., Myles, B. S., Byrd, S. E., Ganz, J. E., et al. (2004). *Autism spectrum disorders: Intervention and treatments for children and youth.* Thousand Oaks, CA: Corwin Press.

Smith, T. (2001). Discrete trial training in the treatment of autism. *Focus on Autism and Other Developmental Disabilities, 16*(2), 86–92.

Taylor, B. A., & McDonough, K. A. (1996). Selecting teaching programs. In C. Maurice, G. Green, & S. C. Luce (Eds.), *Behavioral intervention for young children with autism: A manual for parents and professionals* (pp. 63–177). Austin, TX: PRO-ED.

Van Meter, L., Fein, D., Morris, R., Waterhouse, L., and Allen, D. (1997). Delay versus deviance in autistic social behavior. *Journal of Autism and Developmental Disorders, 27,* 557–569.

Person being observed: _____ Date: _____

+ = achieved   − = not achieved   N/A = not able to observe

Goal	Achieved?	Notes
The instructor completes a reinforcement assessment before working with the student.		
Appropriate materials and reinforcers are ready before the session begins.		
If appropriate: The instructor provides the student with the choice of a larger reinforcer to be gained at the end of a *successful* teaching session.		
The instructor maintains student motivation by providing *appropriate* (smaller amount for lesser demands, etc.) reinforcement.		
The instructor reinforces the student only for correct responses.		
When the instructor provides reinforcement, it is *immediately* after the correct response.		
The student cannot reach reinforcers or gain reinforcement except through the instructor.		
If using tangible reinforcement, the instructor provides specific praise along with the reinforcer.		
Overall, the session is positive and fun.		

Person being observed: _____   Date: _____

+ = achieved   − = not achieved   N/A = not able to observe

Goal	Achieved?	Notes
The instructor does not place demands on the student when initially pairing with him or her.		
The instructor offers access to reinforcers in small amounts to increase the frequency of interaction with the student.		
The instructor offers access to reinforcers that the student cannot access independently (can obtain only through the instructor).		
The instructor does not interrupt the student while he or she is engaging in a reinforcing activity (unless it is time to end the activity).		
The student allows the instructor to play next to him or her and occasionally touch or play with the same items.		
The instructor ends the session on a positive response.		
Overall, the session is positive and fun.		

Person being observed: _____   Date: _____

+ = achieved   − = not achieved   N/A = not able to observe

Goal	Achieved?	Notes
The instructor and the student pair successfully, and the student views the instructor as a reinforcer (does not try to run away).		
Initially, the instructor provides reinforcement for every instruction.		
At first, the instructor provides easy requests (S^D) and instructions.		
The instructor provides appropriate amounts of reinforcement to maintain the strength of the reinforcer.		
The instructor maintains control of the reinforcers; access to reinforcement is only through the instructor.		
The instructor avoids presenting S^Ds that compete with any existing reinforcement that is occurring.		
The instructor increases the number and difficulty of tasks gradually over time; more is required of the student for the same amount of reinforcement.		
The instructor ends the session on a positive response.		
Overall, the session is positive and fun.		

Person being observed: _____ Date: _____

+ = achieved   − = not achieved   N/A = not able to observe

Goal	Achieved?	Notes
Appropriate materials and reinforcers are ready.		
The student is appropriately positioned and oriented toward the instructor and materials.		
The student is positioned so that distractions in the environment are minimized.		
The instructor maintains a high level of success by mixing easier and more difficult tasks.		
The instructor maintains student motivation by providing appropriate reinforcement.		
The instructor presents a sufficient number of trials per session.		
The instructor ends the session on a positive response.		
Overall, the session is positive and fun.		

Person being observed: _____   Date: _____

S^D	Prompt Type	Faded? (Y/N—how?)	Response Correct? (Y/N)	Notes
1.				
2.				
3.				
4.				

Person being observed: _____   Date: _____

+ = achieved   − = not achieved   N/A = not able to observe

Goal	Achieved?	Notes
The instructor mixes new S^D/skill with mastered skills.		
The instructor does not require a behavior that has not yet been displayed by the student.		
The instructor reinforces all approximations.		
The instructor provides the highest level of reinforcement for the most independent response.		
The instructor ends the session on the most independent response.		
Overall, the session is fun and positive.		

Identify shaping steps (closer successive approximations): _____

_____

_____

Person being observed: _____   Date: _____

+ = performed   − = not performed   N/A = not able to observe

Step Within Procedure	Performed?	Notes
The instructor presents the S^D with the correct answer as a prompt (until the correct response is made by the student).		
The intructor uses the least intrusive prompts.		
The instructor fades prompts appropriately.		
The instructor provides the original unprompted S^D before proceeding to a distracter trial.		
The instructor presents an easy distracter trial.		
The instructor restates original S^D after the distracter trial.		
The instructor returns to the original unprompted S^D before the end of the session.		

Note. If initially the student fails to respond, the instructor repeats the S^D first to ensure that the student is attending.

About the Editor and Author

Richard L. Simpson is professor of special education at the University of Kansas. He currently directs several federally supported projects to prepare teachers and leadership professionals for careers with children and youth with autism spectrum disorders. Simpson has also worked as a teacher of students with disabilities, a psychologist, and an administrator of several programs for students with autism. He is the former editor of the professional journal *Focus on Autism and Other Developmental Disabilities* (published by PRO-ED) and the author of numerous books and articles on autism spectrum disorders.

Sonja R. de Boer is a board-certified behavior analyst (BCBA) and obtained her PhD in special education, with an emphasis in autism spectrum disorders, from the University of Kansas. She has more than 10 years of experience working with students with ASD. She currently works as a consultant regarding interventions for students with ASD. She also provides ongoing consultation for the Psychology Department at Trinity College in Dublin, Ireland, for the development of inclusion programs for students with Asperger syndrome and autism. She has cowritten articles and chapters about the inclusion of students with ASD and is a coauthor of the book *Autism Spectrum Disorders: Interventions and Treatments for Children and Youth.*